"In *Alt-Nature,* we are dropped into tender valleys of intimacy. We move through the violence of relations between self and collective. We navigate the implications of maintaining order and hierarchies through our choices. We emerge wondering if we were happy, if it was joy. After a while, we realize that through these topologies, Saretta has marked ways of imagining a liberating landscape that is yet to come." **—Youmna Chlala**

"*Alt-Nature* feels like a search party for the haunted, the story of a collective body, a nomenclature of ache for belonging through the geographic (and seismic) shifts and social calibration that toggles between the intimate and the structural. A document of desire to be read and re-read. Within this homage to the humanitarian aid worker and to the border crosser who often does not arrive as intended, Morgan moves the reader with her acuity for the precise image steeped in the blooming succulence and necropolitical dynamics that dictate the deserts of Central and Southern Arizona." **—Raquel Gutiérrez**

"What is perspective without a horizon? What grave, no matter how old, is not fresh? What is the most precise language for what the government does to our bodies? Do wounds, do stitches, become part of the body? In the land, of the land? Is love waking up? Breaking earth? How much afterlife can a body bear? These are questions I find myself asking, or being asked, while reading Saretta Morgan's vigilant, exacting, extraordinarily tender book-length indicator species, *Alt-Nature.*" **—Brandon Shimoda**

"What is love set against and within austerity? Not the sudden lushness of oasis, but a discipline. Saretta Morgan's keen-whetted *Alt-Nature* traces intimacies through severe stations—the military, border deserts, the Anthropocene—and finds/maps there the alterity of Black thought and life, which is to say, disciplines sharpened in harsh space-time. As I read and re-read Morgan's forceful collection, I find looseness and humor in nevertheless taut syntax, unease in certainty, shade in her generosity. This is etho-poetry as much as ecopoetry, an exacting meditation on what it is to cultivate freedom in 'emotional fields of decay.' *Alt-Nature* is utterly gorgeous and, for readers committed to the labor of loving hard despite precarity and scarcity, utterly necessary." **—Douglas Kearney**

ALT-NATURE

ALT-NATURE

SARETTA MORGAN

COFFEE HOUSE PRESS

Minneapolis

2024

Coffee House Press books are available to the trade through our primary distributor, Consortium Book Sales & Distribution, cbsd.com or (800) 283-3572. For personal orders, catalogs, or other information, write to info@coffeehousepress.org.

Coffee House Press is a nonprofit literary publishing house. Support from private foundations, corporate giving programs, government programs, and generous individuals helps make the publication of our books possible. We gratefully acknowledge their support in detail in the back of this book.

LIBRARY OF CONGRESS CATALOGING-IN-PUBLICATION DATA

Names: Morgan, Saretta, author.
Title: Alt-nature / Saretta Morgan.
Description: Minneapolis : Coffee House Press, 2024.
Identifiers: LCCN 2023032869 (print) | LCCN 2023032870 (ebook) | ISBN
   9781566896979 (paperback) | ISBN 9781566896986 (epub)
Subjects: LCGFT: Poetry.
Classification: LCC PS3613.O74836 A78 2024 (print) | LCC PS3613.O74836
   (ebook) | DDC 811/.6—dc23/eng/20230920
LC record available at https://lccn.loc.gov/2023032869
LC ebook record available at https://lccn.loc.gov/2023032870

PRINTED IN THE UNITED STATES OF AMERICA

31 30 29 28 27 26 25 24   1 2 3 4 5 6 7 8

For Wendy Jo

I want to wake every morning into love,
where love is the question of *how I'm going to help you get free,*
where that means whatever it needs to mean.

Contents

ALT-NATURE

We had very good reason to believe that the authorities were lying. Were not omnipresent. Which meant the authorities would at some moment arrive.

The thing we knew: *to see clearly, and to think clearly—that is, dangerously—and to answer clearly the innocent first question:*

And still, we carried concealed on the highways.

We hushed the horses' mouths.

We put our heads to the horses' mouths. So we wouldn't be lonely.

Now in coming between one desert
and another, I recognize the edges, parting and clear.

I dip my hand into the bath
      over your hair.

I ask you not to shave.

I ask, *open the error.*
      And skin blades open the river.
      And your great eye opens over a ruined field.
      From here geography extends a labored pulse.

More music, palmed casings. This love story a horse still drunk from
war, where I am the incredible absence of her jaw. A soft pink gaining.

      You say Dearth is no name for a horse.

Here, how she rises
from every pussing wound.

The officers gouge jasper eyes
from the mud. I love you.

     …

Dearth, irrational, makes empty the valley. From elongated shadows, pulp of her desire.

When this happens we must love ourselves fiercely, the ancestors and lost humans declared.

The human who was wearing the hat of a particular sports team.

The human who dropped their hair comb.

The human who thought she would reach Utah by Tuesday.

Only deserts witness the slow and complete life of water.

A story of chassis. And foraged box springs.

The one sound offered wandering night without horizon.

Each exceeds its genre while remaining truly intact.

...

This epic has no hero but flesh
           which defies imagination.

The carrion large birds fear, ambulant and calling your name.

Foregrounding and comments for what hinges beyond a thorough wound:

Likely to suffer, my gift stumbles graft with sores.

      Bring me the officer's music.

Bring me the landscape gouged from your eyes.

      …

Low-basin flora. Verdant.
       Inching vertebral ache.

A warm anatomy to feel threatened;
                    endangered by;
                    thick-muscled and in danger of. Iridescent over.

       And in the tissue between floodplains and the officer's science.
And the quiet between and want for shade, the hooded eyes and fluid
body.

Gentle body for whom I lie down.

       . . .

Tonight I walk the dog, committing to memory the darkened color and shape of each car to pass.

So it must have been for the first stars to harvest light from what they followed.

I've placed a shotgun on layaway. A service I haven't used since I was twelve. Having unlearned to be ashamed of needing time or not knowing how to use it.

Knowing the distension harbored in the officer's heart. (Perceiving it through its disciplinary veils.)

The horse stamps out from waxy brush. Viral smell in the cuts up her thighs,

Tell me, baby duck, your wrecked unsleeping door.

...

Love, if you are where I am.

>   *Even your smallest of errors.*
>   *Your most wrecked door.*

The rock faces are opened.

The genres are all up for aerial eradication.

To the forty-yr-old fish. To the abundant bufflehead and ring-necked ducks drifting south across the sunset. I love you.

            …

In the beginning there was the we [. . .] *we* being the most intimate and
also the most political form of accessing one's subjectivity.

—Cristina Rivera Garza, *Grieving*

The sharp calls advancing across the valley were no longer for us.

Or they would be again, but not yet. Stretching yards and deserts in their weight.

Though we could name the places and their capitals. We could pull a needle through every orifice long and small.

Water falling is the sensual conflict of a heart split open. We felt for every boundary, adjacent to which neighboring vertebrates fed themselves.

A simple degree toward the wrong coordinate and the moment could change completely. And the change would be thoroughly complete. Would ring through the bones of our appearance.

A thoroughly surrounding contraindicative pulse.

The voices advancing, in some instances observing our fear, accelerated the physical expression of hours. Publicly. In suggestive incongruent thrusts.

We slept through the engine-braking. The conflicting nightmilk intrusions. Woke morning after morning to swarms of fruit-sucking bees. They too on their way downriver to welcome the morning in a good way.

Tender ensembles to articulate the water's edge.

We woke to the doorframe at the edge of dunes, which we'd always believed was a metaphor. But there ajar along the sagged sand fencing.

We said this with care, though the sagging was one of hostility. We said, Someone should fix that.

Little passed through the frame

The pussing stitches

The counter stitches

The stitched rosettes

Tenderness surrounding their appearance

Tenderness indicating an introduction

A growing necessity to debride

We followed our intentions. Swaying. Soft with desire on the tails of the processions whose shoulders did not rise above the brush.

Our intentions pleated in such a way that our intentions could neither be challenged nor brought entirely to light.

Their tenderness veiled by the inversion of light.

Doubt, our precise and technical transformation.

Of all the things we didn't know:

The most efficient way to release a dog's bite is to—we never would've guessed—put a finger in its ass. Which demonstrates clearly the importance of context with regard to appropriate behavior.

Context was what we waited for.

These conflicts in passing accumulated in the moment for which we prepared.

Though when it arrived we were wet.

We were wide eyed and well read. Waiting.

Readiness, we realized, was never the appropriate goal.

A language of subordination that privileges lung capacity holds my
head up to its yellowing chest

How simple recovery appears from the vista emerging a grammar that
stumbles wearily among the trees,

The encounters surface with brutality, and agitated,

My shoulders surface marked with institutional feeling, awareness comes
and alternately explains and is not who I am,

Deep-rooted impressions from which a definite source arrives,

Standing in line for azaleas, pulled to the ground when it rains,

Some mornings the mist over everything,

Light glaring and indirect as the vehicles were cleared,

This feeling is clear, then the words that have left my face,

The mountain line, its language verbatim, directed at no one,

Prompted in desire to move forward,

Speech to avoid formation of awareness when touching in attitudes made
common,

Its consequences obstruct arrival as they arrange in the field,

In which I believe the source my face encounters,

The woods in which one has no business,

Locations to bodies to jurisdictions stripped of grass, where distress made a territory of its rise to repeat the morning,

The mornings I remembered the field I remembered,

Unresolved verbiage, enough to remain at the appropriate range,

Or run, a minor expression of remembering performed especially in the mornings,

Running was asking for not this one nor this one,

For flatter abs and a thigh gap, while my fitness was measured in readiness to drag a human's weight,

The most loved being the body that re-emerges without need,

Slick roots appear en route to the clearing, then hell is characterized by your temperature upon entering,

Languages of immobilization rose up this way always hungry and for the most lowly thing,

Which is to say that if you could say it once,

Repeating the information by hand:

Information leading to the correct block, arranged by height, on the second of three available channels at two a.m.,

I didn't say I would rather be dead than sleep,

Or that language was reproducing my estrangement, all the maps and surficial refrains,

Eventually terms come to surface in their light,

Explicit, irrefutable,

I said to myself, *you are,*

My uniform reflected in vending machine plexi, *You are, you're going to hell,*

Or, I was staring down the produce aisles, no vegetable vibrant or most appealing,

The mornings chewing slowly until all the eyes went dark.

Suddenly, it felt, everyone was deploying to Africa,

Black people I knew and didn't know were expressing romanticism
without a lick of irony in their tone,

Whether sounds were frequent or unexpressed,

Whether water across exposed corneas, or philosophical prepositions
grasping at dawn,

Hesitation materially unannounced between the lengths of knowing
light,

From words used in an obvious conventional way, the basic red edge
swelling,

Say it again, *the longer the mouthful, the closer to God,*

Say you're from Canada, I was told in Cyprus, where they took my
passport,

But I didn't think then, bringing my hand to the mouth of a sailor's
almost-bride,

I embodied the tradition, I was tiptoeing into the gray-cast sea,

The sand laced with feral cats, torn branches of eucalyptus like
embroidery, aromatic,

Whereas origins are structured by the body's temperature upon entering,

Which is a geographic belief to map sufficient desire,

To produce enough distance,

Or maintain the everyday fantasy of extremism in the bush,

Whereas *territory* could be anything, clarification on a sound,
measurable trust,

Shaking the handle because there are more ways to watch someone die,

More bright, memorable faucets in the hall.

My parents used to tell us: *I'll give you something to cry for.*

A threat seen clearly from its bruised root is pointless.

The root, a deeply harmonic, deeply probing desolation in the nerves and intention.

It renders an individual gift moot.

My dad shared this story.

He arrived, an Army recruiter, to pick up a new enlistee. A Native kid outside Albuquerque. Everyone in the house began to cry. More people arrived, filling the tight space, and they cried too. Before long my dad was crying with them.

I asked him what had he been crying for. And he looked at me like I was a fool.

They're no less stunning, their colors no less luminous, the afternoons in which each decision dangles a gnarled and obvious charm.

The obvious being a baseline. Or borderline
within which I may already feel.

But they're different when you're not a man. The consequences.

Do I regret my time in the military, my mom wants to know.

There's a lot I regret but nothing rises until I say so.
It rises from a position that stalks and orients its path
through broken things by regret.

What I've passed behind. Always asking the wrong
question.

Little buds of wild lavender.

Groundbirds blanketed with grasses on the other end. What underlies
the encounter is soft and falls apart.

The foundation. Not a spatial placement but scale that loves our quota.

Our vocabularies of loss.

The love that is load-bearing.

The love that waits.

Expectation knots the surface of its calloused palm.

The obvious, endangered. Not-involuntary reactions.

Such as the clear expression of want.

We are two women in public. One still believing it's possible to control whether someone looking can look and think "nigger" or not.

Albuquerque was the first time he'd had an affair.

My mom can say this now without any pain.

> This is how she shows me: take on the mantle of defining
> yourself.

There are interludes between us.

Degrees of softness that go unnoticed.

Dear darkness. Dear hemorrhage. The tender blue holes concentrate with light.

Holes like decades. Advancing with acute, unannounced release

the lip of geologic faults.

I say I want to share something.

And it doesn't have anything to say about you.

> We are two hearts moving shoulder to shoulder. Dear
> hungry moon above our heads.

> I say my goodness if you don't relax your neck. I'll chicken out.

For Francees, because she said, One day maybe you'll write a poem
about us

For a long time she could make a living weaving dream catchers from
paper beads and wild bird feathers in her birthplace, Agua Prieta.

She could call from detention to remind me of my anniversary. Of
my wife's birthday, weeks before the fact. I'd say, Whose birthday is it
coming? But she was never wrong.

In that life she said, I must be patient with my daughter.

Offered anything she would say, I want my mom.

In this life she tells the police they're thugs. They're just like them. Or cowards. She gets run out of the city, which is where her mother says she must wait. Her mother says, You've been on the streets before.

Injury pins each heart to the appropriate scale, and an injured heart doesn't step onto the same street twice.

But the pigeons walk the city map missing whole feet or toes.

She calls from the phone of the friend who sells cotijas. Who works in a maquiladora, and weekends sells baked goods from disposable bags.

See the afternoon sweating.

Here, a blue ring she holds to her eye.

The hauled pomegranates have stained her chest.

She returned to Agua Prieta to find the wall wrapped in foil by an artist, so that when the sun began to set the distinctions disappeared. So that she said, Oh, I think I see. And she said, Growing up it was never like this, though I ran through the wall to get from school to the house I was born in.

To go from that home to be with my mom when the wall was a fence or a joke we used to get home faster.

And her shoulder was restless against my shoulder. And we walked to the store for a Coke.

In the background the officers dragged old tires across the sand.

In this foreign city the population is small. Very few spend money on beads & pigeon feathers.

She takes care of a man. It is the same job her mother does.

She walks the dogs.

Cleans out the fridge, which nearly gives him a heart attack.

The dogs he named Pandemia y Pandemia.

¿Me habrías mirado? he says to her.

The geriatric coyote. She responds with a joke.

"—the child, as currently conceptualized, is scalar force made productive.

&

Who can have access to the protection of childhood remains central to the articulation of racializing economies of governmentality.

&

It has similarly relied on a practice of shredding affective relations to build and maintain a labor force."

Mary Pat Brady,
Scales of Captivity: Racial Capitalism and the Latinx Child

A white mother sets the scale for injury:

Demeter raided the earth. Fields scorched in her agony. While another woman's grief doesn't manifest in economicological devastation but is compounded by it.

The concentrations of displaced labor.

Dust under the door. American factories. IMF relief.

Demeter had the privilege to be overcome. She had a Lover-God. And groves and men to absorb her hunger.

The Demeter Coyote: In a land of vaginas, where you have but one, your country must be small.

Too small to move within.

The Daughter Coyote: I know I must be patient with this nation.

The Agent Coyote: This is the joke.

Your life isn't special or imminent except in the inch of land before you will be assaulted.

It doesn't matter where you grew up from age two and went to school and birthed your baby; still you have to go home. Or at least not here.

Her every attempt to return has been documented. The lawyer pushes worn folders across his desk. Hermes in a Men's Wearhouse suit. He says the Ninth Circuit has been consistent.

The Lawyer-God. The Ox-Eyed God. God of Shields. Those of lesser stature. How many Gods are needed to articulate the economy of death.

And the women turned to fountains. Bone dry. The women breathing, rust-overtaken.

The Calliope Coyote: In conditions of violence in spite of their very specific design.

The Geriatric Coyote: You'll leave like the others do.

The Persephone Coyote: I emerged in the reins shaken.

(The other way around.)

Though we arrive at once, we take joy alone.

And in that aloneness, I love her.

Driving with my dog along the border I remembered a line from the lawyer's file and I could hear her in my head. The steel beams ticked by. It was:

> *Because I wanted to be with my mom.*

The governing scale:

The nation-contoured wilderness. From which at the end of the day I drive myself home.

The regulatory scale:

That her daughter would slap her in a room of polycarbonate mirrors and women.

The limited scale:

I said, Well, four hours is a long drive. It was the one time she's looked at me like that.

"Scale is also a powerful epistemological form, neither neutral nor transparent.

&

Western imaginary organizes an understanding of spatial and social relations, that is, as the merely logical way to describe being-in-place.

&

Spatial scaling demonstrates the shaping, capturing force of scale."

Mary Pat Brady,
Scales of Captivity: Racial Capitalism and the Latinx Child

Pandemia y Pandemia consume what's left of the coffee and what was intended for lunch.

The Persephone Coyote: The century rings into its own jagged ear.

The Geriatric Coyote offers to buy ice cream when his government check comes in.

It arrives to the nephew who operates a rancho outside of town.

Though Demeter was encouraged by her Lover-God to look generously
on their daughter's situation, she slaughtered the cattle and farmers alike.

Rivers lifted their heads in love for her. Raised the young girl's torn
girdle in their streams.

Where is the evidence of brutality and threat,
                    is the line that emerges where accountability will not.

The Geriatric Coyote: I know they haven't been paying you.

Occasionally the old man has friends. Those afternoons they lift coca to his face behind the door.

Who am I to say, she says, what an old man in diapers can do.

Her mother wakes directly across the border. In Douglas, AZ, which some mornings could be the world's opposite end. She goes to work. Raises her granddaughter, who wishes to be a nurse.

The Mother Coyote: What will you do when I'm not here.

Okay, she says, do that.

We woke into the morning undressed. Every thought washed of color and their chains rusted over.

Wind howled and fell and whispered beneath the brush. And we with it, bottoming on purpose. But that was not our gift.

Without softness. Without thesis. It was difficult to understand the reach of the occasion or to whom we owed the honor.

Our only meaningful thought flooded crevices of pain.

Pain that was simple. Fundamental as the air before rain.

The circumstances formed around our suffering decayed from the point of initiation inward. This so abandonment became common.

We trained our ears to wake and comprehend the hour. Deliver oxygen. Rest one foot in its light.

We rose our heads only to say, fuck learnedness. Behavior that could only exist in the mouth acquired by failure.

Articulate and reform the needle drawn up into the roof of its suffering.

We weren't going back—not one night, we said—to that disease-shaded landscape. That puss in sheep's clothing, though desire was tied to its awning.

Context required no record. Met us squarely in our eyes.

The eye that awned.

The loud, immeasurable eye.

The eye hugging the feet of our failure required a trust that could only be offered between streams. Or given in the rivers that fed themselves.

We woke with dreams pulled through a fine, intelligent point.

This thorn was a fundamental characteristic of our sides.

History was outlined in our ruin of stitches, re-scaled specifically as though we weren't there.

Language returned through the appearance of clouds. Furtive. Deeply shadowed and offering nothing.

We stood adjacent. Looked up and rubbed our arms.

While not offensive, it's inappropriate to remain in the procession and offer nothing. Not shade nor rosettes. No part in restoring the fence. Neither the most obvious: rain.

We should start a committee, someone said. THE COMMITTEE TO COMBAT LANGUAGE THAT DOES NOT OFFER RAIN, of which the goals and bylaws would be as erotic as they were without a single tooth.

We woke to vandalism relative to the committee.

Someones it seemed were, in their quiet nighttime way, against what they interpreted as the public shaming of nonproductive existence.

For the first time in memory, accountability was on the table. It was bulbous and moist. It absorbed all of the blame, which was not at all called for. It said, I have introduced ideological context.

I ruined the stitches.

I don't feel seen.

I'm absorbed by failure.

I drink from the river and feel nothing.

My gaze depletes.

It is me to whom you owe great honor.

If skin passes always through language, texture is compelled
by desire

If one scar rots the length of an afternoon.

Then morning opens our chests to another science. Delicately
scaled. Veined in silence.

I rest my head on the frame of a burning question. And the future bends
down

from its fine-grained neck. Breathing.

The dominant orientation is based in devotion. The geography, devoted, disfigures each wrist.

Veins negotiate a well-marbled music of territory.

Militant roots open to the half-drawn beauty of corridors. Where the governing image branches with light.

Devastating,

      light passes through a moment, which doesn't mean the moment
ends.

            The moment continues with clarity. We therefore
         will call our transformations "darkness," the proposals
        for which being
            precise, and
            drawn toward the heart.

I release a trigger and rounds emerge, pale wounds from the berm.

Even this sound our valley impresses. Even the futures of thorned
perennials bend.

                        Always underneath it.

         I want language for what the government did to
        my body.

The officers watched lengths of our street. Our legs

were barely covered.

Our streets closed and opened to frame the process of intimate
regard.

Arousing. Delicately lobed.

Bare repulsion blossoming anything you might
ask for.

We studied the houses from their ugly numbered orifices.

The same in Panama. Kentucky. As no contractor ever had another idea.

Hypothetically

I raised my hand.

A bruise re-drawn. Withdrawn from the door jammed
with heat.

Heat of a particular style forced open.

Devastating,

     the hanging weight.

Concerts of landlessness rehearsed in lesioned blooms. Their fruit never fully introduced.

     Listen to the territory open the bright, hot door.

Daily we waited at the barricaded roads. The tinted glass of half-drawn windows.

Having always to be reminded: if you don't stop smiling, I swear.

We watched for the forms through which understanding passed,

proxy to the conditions from which it emerged, drawing intelligence.

Such a simple thing. Every story holds a collective body

amorously or otherwise.

The name lost arrives under the knees of an idea.

No. We're going to do it this way.

We're going to fill our lungs up with (the darkest) juice.

Walking to the corner store on behalf of so-and-so

drenched in possibility

we shaded our curious faces.

The increasing aftermath of repulsion is arrival. (Is a third-party contract and every nigga left holding the bag.) One impression restrained, another will assume the terminal point.

When we reference this hour it holds no reward. Nor does it face away. The fibrous connective tissue mounts:

> Our eyes nearly covered. Our legs cold, we woke with the straightforwardness of being Black regardless of what happened after.
>
> The order's warm
>
> retching fever of—

> it is how scale emerges.

If a sentence passes always-through landscape and that landscape is not vacant, texture by this sentence forms a discursive core.

Psychologically, physiologically, this scar along my thigh.

And from being broken, a science. This murderous clarity we cannot withstand.

Listen how the officers have paused

for the territory to arrive.

The darker the berry

the longer there is to wait.

We will ask you to welcome what arrives.

We embrace it ourselves, having never seen its raw or rotund form.

Acceptance is an orientation. Mapped along the consciousness that rises in our sleep. Toward the faceless choice that does not return us here.

The old conflicts emerged through the feet of the new conflicts. Marks across our bodies branched. All the ways there are to stand in one place. On a mountain. At the bus stop. Offering a single ragged fruit.

A visceral redding eye, context arrived without horizon. Lowered by an octave. Shot through with feeling and mourning from every hole.

A reservoir to one side, the context arrived with an animal in its mouth. It further proposed the geography.

To foil the context was to outrun the authority's imagination. And to refuse all explanations of why what we felt was not real.

To disarm the wolf every time at every gate. Unthread its learnedness and don the lonely pelt.

Scale intimacy like a door. The ambient condition clawing along the rails.

The same bird never appeared twice. Figures disappeared beneath terms and stones under which overturned there was always a little scat.

It wasn't not beautiful.

But the climates might surrender us. Saying only:

    I'm sorry for the way I am.

There were the climates from which we were evacuated.

The climates for which authorities could give two fucks. In which we could not walk to the store.

The dawning climate that was not a horizon but virus steeped inside our bones.

The circulatory climates. Where we were perpetually inappropriately dressed.

Contextual differences didn't occur within the interior. There were no climates within the climates, they occasioned equivalent decay.

This too wished for a name. Dilation to demonstrate the needle's fine, circuitous route. To give respect where respect was due.

We produced gestures to anchor its teeth to our tables. Direct its ankles to the comfort of our love.

Faceless and ragged, the conditions behaved strangely, we liked to say. Though in fact it was duplicitously. The conditions behaved duplicitously but required all our love.

We clenched our fists, yet said:

Have the champagne.

We are figuratively accountable.

Here, let us run to the store.

Have leather.

Eames and designer floors. Designer flowers.

The gun cabinet is designed accordingly. Lovingly custom to order.

Here, allow us to regard the hour.

The problem we wanted to address emerged primarily from our situation

The future appeared   Governed yet conscious of pleasure within our view

Definition bore a flesh rivers widened through
the valley

Each time it rose or ripened

We were the detritus   And chose to aggregate or uncouple

If it were impossible to move past the point of death there wouldn't be
death   But language picked from our bone sockets

All this mapped through a story of desire

Miles and seed to flood a cry or unknown color

                              The bright, horned length of our bodies

                         Which were not seen through language

               But sweat between our breasts

             A narrative ecology   Lonely and expressive
                                                 with nowhere to go

Having digested all the necessary scholarship

Advanced perfect analyses of trauma from inch after inch of receding splendor

We crouched just beyond legible feeling   To undo
gently

A little soft-headed something to at the end of the day unfold from

And though in most scenarios the territory did not break

Our necks rotated to absorb the alienable score

No matter how weaponized the terrain

The music from wash to shaded wash

Where the quiet of feral animals fell against our backs

Our vertebrae unclasped with need

To tell us something

From a very deep place

The cries were a color unfading

Through the splendor   Our mouths were last to disappear

Upon return everything left was
unopened, consumed by humans,
destroyed by humans, or animalized.

One hopes the bees, hiving,
dying in foul-smelling clumps
are not *Africanized*.

The increasing aftermath of invasion.

The wounds, amber-overtaken
near-lovely in the morning.

The first recorded dead
remained unidentifiable to the officers. Lost to exposure.

What to do with a Negro in the desert. Or all of them after.

In dry orchards out of season.

Among cotton.

Saguaro picked by wrens.

Exposure precedes the realization
of an identity or fact.

State of being exposed
to contact with something else.

                              Even when making very little noise.

The soldiers.

Pissing behind creosote. Or elegant
on their horses lined to enter the corral.

Entering each morning before the mountain
silhouettes. A cold hand to unlace the erroneous
and unfortunately pussing stitch.

The hand incorporated along
emotional fields of decay.

The chain cholla fruit then fall. Soil
in Sonora softens according to the rain.

Offering every explanation in full.
Without saying shit. Without gentleness
or stepping back from the officers' science.

Or from how white supremacist they really are.

At the center of the explanation
sits a small box. And to this box
the beetle larvae arrive to feed.

Among legal understandings
of Natural Life in the United States is
the sentence.

As in, for the length of one's natural life.

(There, standing. The distance
of their body to a door cracked
alone in the desert. Irrefutable music.)

The sentence of Natural Life, unlike the sentence
of Life, doesn't allow for the possibility of parole.

Which was anyway discontinued in Arizona in 1993 when the possibility
of parole was replaced with that of release. A process that remains
judicially vague.

Among peoples in the United States
Indigenous peoples are incarcerated
at the highest rates per capita.

          Among Blacks the carceral industry
               (regardless the branching of orchards and
               centuries of trees)
          finds its critical mass.

Every sentence harbors a unique end. That is its gift.
        Night opens a jagged scar.

        Soft purple signals the end
        of night in Southern Arizona.

                        Tree frogs retreat in the depths of winter.
                        Their bodies appear lifeless. As do certain
                        moths

                        that avoid internal freezing by purging
                        their guts.

After the last music.

A man, then unidentified
found FULLY FLESHED; CONDITION CODE 1.

From which water flows north.
PROBABLE ELECTROCUTION
located in a database of migrant deaths.

His coordinates crossed by desert jaguars reliant
on streams.

His coordinates are passed through the beetle's
gentle bowels.

And those of the Bell's vireo.

Identified by a two-part structure.
His definitive response and water
down his slender, grayed breast.

                                              Beneath the cottonwood's
                                              gold-filtered crown.

                    Where the lowland leopard frog remains moist.

                    The large cat's paw print remains fresh in the soil.

After the last music.

Tubman and Whitney hike Brown Canyon. They spot a rare beardless-tyrannulet (did she appear from nowhere?) hugging parched northern boundaries of her species range.

A Mexican jaguar treads backward to observe her melancholic refrain.

It's without their interest that the
Department of Interior studies
effects of stress and fire on vegetation via high-rise
high-res satellite phenomics.

No two droughts are alike.

The earliest Negro recorded dead in Arizona was unidentified.

Having not survived probable hypothermia.
Exposure. Blunt force.

Force accumulates behind the skull
to bear centuries of afterlife and pulp.

The afterlife of being chatteled. Of being made
a glorified mercenary or buffoon.

Hanging naked in the moon's light. Where there is no substitute for the
adjunct feeling.
Coerced into foul-smelling clumps.

Let's say the force requires a hand.
Or an industry. At whatever temperature.
More land.

Let's say some records
are not good.

Or, the pulp is blooming.

And the hands they return
not destroyed exactly
but smelling lonely and of death.

Whether the border looks out from eight hundred and fifty eyes, or two, the MBQ remains few though on the rise

[31.812180, -111.443051]

The boundaries of Buenos Aires National Wildlife Refuge (BANWR) in Southern Arizona were determined in 1985 to facilitate re-introduction of the masked bobwhite quail (MBQ) to a stretch of desert along the US–Mexico border.[1] This charmingly plumed, bottom-heavy, ground-dwelling bird has been designated as an indicator species for the region. This means that based on intensive research on the causal and proxy relationships between overlapping phenomena, the presence or absence of MBQ can be used to assess the vitality of the ecosystem as a whole. As part of a range-wide survey, visitors are asked to report MBQ sightings to the refuge with as much contextual information as is available. However, priorities.

[31.812180, -111.443051]

Between the years 2000 and 2022, the remains of 425 migrant women were publicly recorded in Pima County. Of these, five were found in BANWR. These five were each found on a segment of the refuge's north, east, or west border.

If you look at a map of all the migrant women's deaths recorded in Pima County during this twenty-one-year period (a map in which each woman is represented by a bright red dot), there's an empty refuge-shaped patch in the field of bright red dots.[2] If you find this difficult to visualize, that's appropriate. If you can visualize this, don't take the absence of an image as evidence that the refuge is safe.

[31.812180, -111.443051]

I enjoy camping at BANWR because of the administrative perks afforded to a wildlife refuge. Where national parks necessitate spending on advertising, or amenities such as bathrooms and picnic tables, the refuge budget goes to preserving indicator species, such as the MBQ. The absence of bathrooms, picnic tables, and advertising filters out most people, which is great, as most people camping in southern Arizona are, as a simple matter of statistics, racist and armed to their teeth.

What's unfortunate about the people we do see in the refuge, whether they're white or not, is that nine times out of ten they're Border Patrol, who share a symbiotic relationship with the refuge by maintaining roads—something the refuge cannot afford much to do.

Occasionally at the beginning Nazafarin or I would wave at an agent passing on the road. It wasn't meant to communicate "I'm safe," or "I'm unthreatening and a citizen," but an unfortunate reflex of rural places that surfaced when our guard was down.

[31.779571, -111.560183]

A further notable aspect of the BANWR border occurs at the northwest corner, where the refuge ends, and then approximately half a mile down the road begins again. After turning west off Rt. 286 over a cattle guard and down a decently serviced road, the refuge reemerges in the Baboquivari Mountains to carve out what is known by the US Bureau of Land Management (BLM) as Brown Canyon, a sky island ecosystem accessible November through April by reservation, so long as volunteers are available.

Sky islands are a type of mountain range found throughout the Sonoran Desert. They take their name from a rough metaphor. The high elevation of the mountain is in such contrast with the surrounding low desert that species thriving at the mountain tops would never make it in the surrounding lands. These species are, in a sense, stranded. Though, generally speaking, they aren't stranded until they need to leave.

Just west of Brown Canyon is Baboquivari Peak, a steady accumulation of centuries and magnificent cliff face which, in the Tohono O'odham tradition, is where everything begins.

[31.763821, -111.472797]

The construction is simple. Someone digs a trench. A grate is laid over the trench. Bar spacing of the grate must not allow a large-hoofed animal to pass safely from one side of the trench to the other. Vertical clearance of the grate must not allow an animal to lift itself from the trench once they've stepped between the bars. In addition to barbed fencing, these cattle guards line Rt. 286 along the west border of BANWR.

Why so much (and so little) concern over rogue cows?

Open-range cattle ranching was a major player in the destruction of habitat suitable for MBQ. Introduced by settlers in the mid-nineteenth century, cattle thrived on what until then had been miles and miles of fertile grassland (MBQ habitat of choice). It was too many cattle, and poorly thought out. Before long, this error was exposed by miles and miles of sun-bleached bones.

The cattle that didn't die during the mid-nineteenth-century drought tore the land down to its earth. This was/is a serious problem. Barren earth doesn't possess sufficient fuel to support natural wildfires or controlled burns. In the absence of fires, thriving brush and mesquite prevented the return of grasses. In the absence of grasses, ranchers planted additional trees. In the absence of grasses, when the rains returned there was nothing to hold the land back from the arroyos one sees opening the landscape today.[3]

Standing in the park's northern territory, I find it difficult to visually reconstruct a prior ecological identity. The stressed vegetation and eroding soils adhere closely to American cultural mythologies of parched desert wilderness in need of white-supremacist protection. I say to my dog, Federica: This, lady, is where we practice faith. We believe that the world was different. We believe that it can be different again. Our part in this process is an anxiously evolving question.

[[.], [- .]]

The difficult thing. And this difficulty is ambient, can be non-impressive. The difficult thing about imagining a prior ecological identity is that so much of my imagination, which is to say also my capacity to arrive, has been formed by and within the conditions on which this tragedy rests.

So much rests. And waits. And reposes physically unchallenged. And is estranged within. And wrests within settler-colonial landscapes.

[32.222874, -110.967530]

Nazafarin moved in her twenties to the US for art school. After years in the Midwest, she relocated to Tucson, where her partner is now a professor. We share a loneliness in this desert that's challenging. Her difficulty moves, in part, through the language of painting:

I knew this geography only through painting and photography. Almost always empty of human presence. And grand. Desert romanticism in line with the eighteenth-century European tradition . . . inviting exploration. Expansion and the settler colonial project . . . The main idea being negative space. What is erased or absent from it needs to be recovered.[4]

We send pictures back and forth as she tends an olive tree. I fix nitrogen with native seeds. The practice of watching things grow distorts my alienation into its own curious bulb. Thick-rooted language and orientation. The self-evolving work to remain alongside Native peoples while geohistorically enmeshed in their absence and ongoing genocidal erasure.

Though the consequences weren't immediately visible, the Gadsden Purchase in 1854 drove a then-invisible boundary through the Tohono O'odham Nation. That policy/line superimposed Venn diagrams of tribal/settler-colonial/international spheres that increasingly criminalize and restrict tribal peoples from caretaking lands, engaging in prayer, and practicing traditional climate-responsive migratory patterns that alleviate environmental stress.

Today the boundary grows increasingly visible in some ways.

Example:

Wall construction

Example:

Israeli-imported Integrated Fixed Tower (IFT) surveillance technology has been installed on and off the reservation. While the intended subjects of observation are migrants, cameras don't know the difference.

Today the scope and consequences reproduce infinitely and not visibly in other ways.

Example:

When it began after 9/11, it was so aggressive that it forced the people not to go out on the land anymore. That is really affecting the health of everybody. The health of the elders—who really need to be out on the land to connect with the plants and with the mountain. From that point on, the children don't see their elders out there, they're not connecting to that part of our life. This forced disconnection to the land is unhealthy because with

the disconnection they lose their language, traditional diet, and
sensitivity to turn to traditional medicine.

—Ophelia Rivas, Tohono O'odham elder[5]

Example:

Saguaros having been torn from their orientation to the sun.

[31.791988, -111.577037]

The BLM asks us to accept that their regulation of the Baboquivari Peak Wilderness (roughly two thousand acres added to the National Wilderness Preservation System in 1990) is for everyone's benefit.

Example:

for the preservation of wildlife, motorized equipment is legally prohibited on all lands federally designated as "wilderness."[6]

To believe that the BLM protects land for everyone's benefit, we must first forget that the Tohono O'odham were always here. Or we must believe that their relegation to the Tohono O'odham reservation was/is a painless process. Or (the BLM's favorite) that they don't exist at all.

[43.472208, -80.542454]

If Black culture is critical culture, what I am suggesting is that perhaps it hasn't come about yet . . .

—Hortense Spillers, on "The Idea of Black Culture"[7]

If it's true (and everything Spillers says is true in one way if not others) that our work is to turn critically from the world, to assume a position by which the earth's impressions arrive in view, if from necessity certain bodies turn quietly to earth,

if the enactment of one environment extracts life from another,

if there's a border where life is no longer possible,

if an indicator species points toward the health of a question, a question of Black culture is: whose body constitutes an environment,

if I imagine sounds that challenge my orientation in the grasses,

if constitution happens in that way, at times the practice of Black culture requires a challenge to my impulses of orientation,

if accumulation positions criticality, we might see us in the ghost tufts of grasses, if I'm unthreatening and a citizen thinking through one word, it would be, what it is that a challenge *releases* to coming together.

[31.484262, -111.461975]

The formal cemetery (belonging to the Garcia Ranch family) is a short distance from the BANWR southern border, which is the northern border of Mexico. The roads in this area are increasingly difficult to drive. On our way to the cemetery we pass several deer and a few birds we haven't seen before. No MBQ.

Standing outside the fence, Nazafarin talks about her youth in northern Iran. These hills are similar to those of her mother's ancestral village. She asks if Federica is allowed in the cemetery, as Federica is sniffing around the graves. I say, Federica Garcia Lorca Elisabeth Morgan-Diaz, if you don't get your Black ass out of there. And she does in her time.

Nazafarin (the painter) and I (the poet) think about how we encounter and express our socio-geographic experiences of southern Arizona. As immigrant. As Black. As woman. As queer. As cis. As citizen, naturalized and not. We stumble through language and subject positions, the web of desires and antagonisms our bodies emerge, upon contact with systematically exploited lands. Lands that still function as long, shallow graves. And that collect a sky so stunning that unless it's you who are dying, you forget at times how fresh they are, the graves.

[31.592359, -111.448734]

Again I'm late and Nazafarin has chosen a campsite. She's chosen this site for its vista, which is indeed impressive. When I arrive, she's reading Etel Adnan in a folding chair overlooking the mountains. She's identified where the ground is soft enough for stakes. I choose a clearing of dirt behind three low mesquite trees, where I anticipate protection from the wind.

My tent is half up when I notice Federica rolling through dead grass between the three trees. She's so into it. Full-body enthusiasm from nose to tail. It's the particular roll, neck first, that she reserves for things that stink. Federica is rolling back and forth over the severed leg of a deer. I say, Federica Garcia Lorca Elisabeth Morgan-Diaz, get your Black ass out of there. I call to Nazafarin to show her what we've found. She says that she remembers having seen it. That she saw it, then quickly un-saw it. I realize that I had too.

Not far from the leg there's another, and a little farther from that, a twisted carcass. We like this spot, so it's the remains that must go. I load them up and drive a few minutes down the road, where I nudge each off the truck bed with my boot.

On my way back to camp, I get an uneasy feeling. I return, to the coarse hair followed down to flaking hooves, and I cover them with what branches are near.

I walk down the hill from our spot for wood. No rain this year, but the downed wood is faintly green at its core. Fresh cut by the rangers. No good for fires. I find more deer legs. Three, and I'm disappointed. You're going to be sleeping in someone's kitchen tonight, my lover tells me when I call her on the phone.

Around the fire we pour wine and listen to coyotes hunt beyond the tree line in howls and yips. We open a pack of cigarettes to observe stars and the moon.

[37.923461, -122.596331]

I feel trapped in this universe and think of what an anti-verse could mean, which is still a universe; there is no way out.

—Etel Adnan, *Journey to Mount Tamalpais*[8]

[40.672736, -73.982974]

What is meant here by perception is a form of listening that transfigures the relation between subject and object, that reaches into layers of history buried underground.

—Omar Berrada on *Journey to Mount Tamalpais*[9]

[[.], [- .]]

I've worked with No More Deaths to provide humanitarian aid in another stretch of the Sonoran Desert (about 130 miles northwest) since 2018. On our way out to drop water at the coordinates we maintain, I don't look up. The trail is unpredictable, shifting as it does with rain. Because water is heavy, my breath pulses in my ears. The chain cholla stand in clusters, small men bearing fruit. Inevitably a cholla pup adheres to my pants. For the first three years my backpack lacks a suspension system. The straps constrict nerves in my neck and shoulders, which produces pain and occasional numbing in my arms. A pain of my own negligence, as I had money and intent to purchase a better one.

On our way back from placing water, the mountains defy my memory. There's no sufficient way to acknowledge the interstitial vacuum between what I see and how the landscape appears without water and satellite GPS, or a truck two miles away, or with policies such as "Prevention through Deterrence" forcing each step into the most circuitous terrain. Here too, faith is no substitute for a systematically limited imagination. The vacuum is incomprehensible. It waits beyond my understanding, in thorns and biological soil crusts. Waiting for someone else even as I enter it.

[32.213466, -110.971526]

Increasingly in this wake of US withdrawal from Afghanistan, Nazafarin mentors Afghani youth in refugee status. I asked her what it's like to hear her language spoken abundantly in these deserts. She replied: It's strange.

[32.538254, -114.558886]

A fellow humanitarian aid worker began a database and map of IFTs across southern Arizona.[10] She submits FOIA requests or skims travel blogs for a general sense of where a tower might be. Then she combs Google Earth for exact visual cues, such as roads smoothed for a tower's installation and service. Or the bright-white cluster of pixels on which each beacon rests.

In real life, they're unmistakable—eighty-foot structures supporting 360-degree radar, night cameras, and a telephone all juiced off a renewable solar battery with propane reserve. Via satellite, the lattice of virtual fencing slips with its data into an angle of shadow so slight at times there is no telling how many.

[31.459365, -111.465157]

From mile twenty we could see variations in a corner of the San
Luis Mountains. An ochre cut across the color time takes for land to
encounter itself. We imagined phenomena and millennia building on top
of one another.

Driving further the next day, approaching the border, we realized the
absence of color was land cleared in order to extend construction. A
transubstantive property of the American West is that it's "wilderness"
until it's not. You can't operate a motor vehicle until you can plow the
land over to build a wall. The BLM has patience, and faith that in time
everything can change.

[31.592359, -111.448734]

I wake to the sound of rustling, perhaps sniffing, outside my tent. I think
maybe a coyote or bobcat. Federica is unbothered, which upsets me, as
I would like to be asleep too. Mountain lions come down this far when
water is scarce. Less than ten miles from the border, it could be cartel, a
possibility the BANWR website clearly states. Worst-case scenario, it's one
of the backward-looking white men who come here to hunt.

The truck's panic button can startle off animals. It might repel humans,
but if not, they'll be ready. I consider a single shot in the air. Warning
shots are illegal. If you truly believe your life is in danger, the only legal
response is to kill. I breathe and listen. I will my bladder to rest.

Illuminated by sunrise, the dirt around my tent is smooth. Without
tracks or signs of disturbance. Nazafarin is out for her morning walk.
She goes off to paint and watch for animals. I'm making cheesy grits
with eggs when she returns. I keep hearing deer, she says, herds of them
running through the trees.

We drive down to the border and east along the wall, weaving through crews of men, water-holding pools, and trucks with tires taller than my head. The packed dirt is red and rises into steep hills. I pause at the top of one, feeling already the drop of it, nearly vertical. Roadrunners slip in and out of the steel beams that divide our bodies from the neighboring State.

We stood in recognition of our particular form. Where in times of crisis the tributaries, osseous and moaning, converged to enter dry ground.

Against abandonment. Orchards. Against analysis, astonishing gorges. Well-coated seed.

But the democratizing force, it was said, is the terror that will always reach you no matter how withdrawn the cavity or breath. There's always something to work with and to refuse a scar.

The voices who said this would then disappear. Poof. Released across trails of afternoon light.

The thesis was unrecognizable: fields in its only color. Mountains eroded to their rims. This had sexual connotations, and actually several forms took place.

Luxurious. Invasive. With byproducts that remained distant and nearly impossible to drain.

Valleys blurred. Made critical the hours that fed only from their depressions. That did not regard learnedness. Or rest in its light.

We observed the cleft faces. The conditions under which each depression was an appropriate place to look.

The sustainable valleys, evident in their fortitude.

The unburdened valleys multiplied into themselves once filled to their rims.

The gorged organic valley. The trampled valley. The bastard valley.

The valley without proper circulation. Without forms that could speak to its diminishing alterity even when the alterity was most observed to be diminished.

Unlike the openings of animals with four legs or two, any perforation obliterated the contents with light.

Stepping out from the orifices, a voice called to us, saying:

To arrive everywhere from nowhere is the one true gift.

Thus, we didn't understand those who were happy to trade their whole consciousness for a luminous horizon. With its clumps and diffusions of literal prison.

For a well-battered corpse. Yet each day its anatomy and consequences grew.

The zen garden is nice on the weekends but the door will lock
behind you

Here we are all thinking and not thinking about being dead,

We fight the dogs from our shoelaces and from each other by holding
their well-decorated vests,

This place is full of bitches though you can't say that, though you're a
person rightfully pissed off,

We don't all want to be heroes,

We don't all want to not die,

Except for this country, we don't want to die for that,

Leaving curved impressions, germinal, with no expectation in return,

Leaving room to acknowledge capitalist patriarchy's broad and coercive
applications,

However meager or capacious the desire, our statistics are inevitably
abused,

Asked again whether I've considered hurting myself or others ever or in
the past two weeks, I make a joke about the future,

Whose companion story dreams itself in the obstacles budding across
every new path to love,

It's that no path to forgiveness would look like this,

I say I'm sorry, yes, I know this isn't funny,

But is also a testimony to the enormous "thing" we do to the extent we
are able,

Forgiveness from who, came a voice from across the room,

How long does it take, if nothing was cut or crushed,

But the day hangs from jangling hooks above your sorry yellowing head,

Three weeks into the prescription I woke thinking THIS . . . is what it
feels like to be white,

No one disagreed,

It didn't make any sense; anyway it didn't last,

The official formulas for suffering are mostly subjective; I've accepted
that I am one who will never suffer enough,

A position both intentionally obscuring and clear,

> The United States was "conceived in slavery" and
> christened by genocide. These early practices established
> high expectations of state aggression against enemies
> of the national purpose—such as revolutionary slaves
> and indigenous peoples—and served as the crucible for
> development of a military culture that valorized armed
> men in uniform as the nation's true sacrificial subjects.
>
> —Ruth Wilson Gilmore, *Abolition Geography,*

None of the signs say thank you for your left arm, or hearing, or lymphatic health, or land,

I want to thank you for being alive,

And thank you, unfortunately, when it isn't what you want to be,

Thanks down to the lines creasing your deeply infatuated head,

I wanted to volunteer for the Vets against War Crisis Hotline,

Then I didn't write back, or attend any medical appointments that year,

I'm disappointed by the cadence of paltry confessions I make in order to keep living,

Later, in the rooms where we can speak, we want to know why do we feel so emotional.

The only time Abou has appeared in an unpleasant dream

I return to my old office where only the furniture has changed. I no longer have a uniform but piece together insignia, careful to wipe puss from the stitches, clean. The officer in charge is dressed in long blue silk and gaudy beads. Abou is there, in dense naturally dyed robes covering his body and face, to assist in ceremony. The man beside him is jealous of the attention I'm receiving from our officer. She invites me to whisper my reflections into her ear while we pass around the medicine, and I agree to because I'm afraid. Later I engage this man along the road. I tell him that he can be less afraid of his fear. He tells me to watch my back. I smile in return so that he can see what I mean. Abou is gone, and this man, he can sense I have no one. Every one of my old colleagues is disgruntled over my return. Especially when I'm discovered dry-humping one of the enemies. I say I'm providing distraction and checking her for weapons. And indeed we are now outnumbered and out-armed. Without the element of surprise and with our internal divisions exposed. My SIG trigger dies, as it's been known to do. Then, miraculously, the moment extends slowly. All eyes shift at the pace of icicle births. I'm able to perform troubleshooting procedures. Still, it's useless. Jerking and sweat ripple the distant edge of my sleep and I'm aware that this edge is not open to me. A dramatic fall in pressure occurs beyond the warehouse walls, it emerges horror in the eyes of our enemies. During their rush to seal off the building, they're unconcerned with us. In the commotion, I alone am left outside.

The revolution will not be televised, yet she turns from the horizon
and is waving hello

What rises first in the wilderness internal to love.

Coming upon a cop vehicle on fire, the question is where to linger.

When to return my eyes.

In light of the most beautiful horizon.

Sleeping with heat by your side, position everything always the same way.

The glock / the cock / the pillow spray in well-spaced formation. Always
the same order.

The key is to continue with clarity.

I stay ready, so I don't never got to get ready, an old friend would say.

But he was talking about film. Visual aesthetics. Here, the bewildered
underlying.

Every light on but all the rooms . . .

I don't never keep. I don't never quickly.

I say, What is it that arrives in you.

Progressive muscle relaxation then I just.

Another worn penny for the sex that doesn't come.

Another mountainside of desert poppies.

Scorched slope of the future that won't return.

And is indiscernible from the center of my hand.

When I get out of bed the air conditioner still isn't working.

And Mingus on vinyl and I demonstrating how to best scramble soft eggs.

Refuge is born in the decision to not die. And to not fight either, in that fatal schema anymore.

We arrived at a breathless edge. An unfortunate relationship to the world.

Gnarling roots evacuated of verbal expression. Survival void of expression that was yet impolite.

The explanations were acceptable and the desert unstoppably green, still old feelings raised their eyes from the dirt.

From the ongoing question, which brushed our arms in velveteen breaths.

Rose the pain of knowing our hope remained intact. Given a language to love us. Balanced between a basic set of possibilities and our choice at any moment to take a back way home.

Each said:

> That I have been so secluded. I held defeat as my own. Is the
> culminating authorial point.

Unnamed in occasions of inconsistent bruising. Internally consequential
terror.

Consequences never not in season. Or at our fingertips. On tap.
Unoccupied. Romantically unengaged.

Sleepless against the wet earth. A lush-eyed animal looking forward with
ragged breasts.

What happened after that.

Memories terminated before our private shelter of consciousness. Fleshed sound over hoof over hand. Marble in the gray-pink sky, an impression that carried no heat. Though its promise was physical.

To be perfectly happy and not strangers to ourselves.

Its promise. That it would find its way back somehow.

We gathered around simulations of the future. Oily skin pulling away from the skull. A tenderness looking back through crepuscular hours.

(Is this the place?)

The simulation of eating a meal together. With tears in our eyes. Carrying on.

Come now. The question rises in everyone. From the base of the neck the world opens, failed. Receptive. Just like that.

The territories we've left behind are all gone now.

The rain falls through them refracting light.

Notes

"Dearth-light" was written in conversation with several poems in Natalie Diaz's *Postcolonial Love Poem,* and through watching and loving a person devoted to the possibilities of language.

—

The recommendation in "Consequences upon arrival (i)" for releasing a dog's bite was offered on a tense morning at Red Lake Treaty Camp by Amber Morning Star Byars (Choctaw), who provided leadership at RLTC in early fall 2021. She was also the first person to offer me a practice of meeting the morning in a good way.

RLTC was one site in a network of camps established by Indigenous water protectors as part of the #StopLine3 movement. In fall 2021, drilling for the pipeline had moved on from RLTC's section of Red Lake River, and the camp was shifting in function to primarily provide a space of ceremony and retreat for water protectors coming from frontline encounters elsewhere. Under Amber Morning Star's guidance, RLTC was a space to think deeply about what it meant to arrive at a place—the needs and consequences of that process. Also about what it meant, from an Indigenous perspective, to feel and create safety. And to prioritize (through ritual and respect) a capacity to dream good.

—

An earlier version of "A horizontal appearance" was commissioned by the Tucson Museum of Art in 2021 to accompany Nazafarin Lotfi's work in the show, *4x4: Willie J. Bonner, Nazafarin Lotfi, Alejandro Macias, and Anh-Thuy Nguyen.*

—

"Dominant orientation lights a corridor wide as Mexico's northern border" references images of African American cavalry in Arizona taken for the Farm Security Administration/Office of War Information Photo Collection held by the Library of Congress. Additionally, information was taken from the Humane Borders Migrant Death Mapping database.

—

"Whether the border looks out from eight hundred and fifty eyes, or two, the MBQ remains few though on the rise," was written for *Dark Soil: Fictions and Mythographies* (forthcoming, Coffee House Press), edited by Angie Sijun Lou and Karen Tei Yamashita.

1. Buenos Aires National Wildlife Refuge, "About Us," U.S. Fish & Wildlife Service (website), accessed August 8, 2022, https://www.fws.gov/refuge/buenos-aires/about-us.
2. "Arizona OpenGIS Initiative for Deceased Migrants," Humane Borders (website), last modified July 2022, https://humaneborders.info/app/map.asp.
3. Buenos Aires National Wildlife Refuge, "About Us."
4. Nazafarin Lotfi, text message to the author, February 2, 2022.
5. Caitlin Blanchfield and Nina Valerie Kolowratnik, "Significant Impact," E-Flux (website), accessed August 8, 2022, https://www.e-flux.com/architecture/at-the-border/325749/significant-impact/.
6. "A Cheatsheet for Demystifying The Wilderness Act Public Law 88-577," United States Department of Agriculture (website), accessed August 8, 2022, https://www.fs.usda.gov/Internet/FSE_DOCUMENTS/stelprdb5313909.pdf.
7. University of Waterloo English Department, "Hortense Spillers: The Idea of Black Culture," YouTube video, 1:25:36, November 24, 2013, https://youtu.be/P1PTHFCN4Gc.
8. Etel Adnan, *Journey to Mount Tamalpais,* 2nd ed. (New York: Litmus Press, 2021), 11.

9. Omar Berrada, "The Undying Vibrancy of All Things" in *Journey to Mount Tamalpais,* 2nd ed. (New York: Litmus Press, 2021), 74.
10. Tara Plath, "Methodology," AZ Beacon Map, accessed August 8, 2022, https://azbeaconmap.org/methodology/.

—

The perspective on readiness in "The revolution will not be televised, yet she turns from the horizon and is waving hello" was shared by filmmaker Elegance Bratton. The title is elaborated from Gil Scott-Heron's "The Revolution Will Not Be Televised." The italicized lyrics mid-poem are taken from Joan Armatrading's "Woncha Come on Home," the first love song to rock my heart.

Acknowledgments

Thank you to Coffee House Press, particularly my editor, Erika Stevens, for believing in what earlier iterations of this book could become.

To Dionne Lee for trusting me with your art for the cover of my dreams.

To Youmna Chlala, Raquel Gutiérrez, Douglas Kearney, and Brandon Shimoda for offering thoughtful reflection.

To the following spaces where language in *Alt-Nature* first appeared: *The Volta, Neck,* the Academy of American Poets *Poem-A-Day* series, (w/ Erica Hunt and TC Tolbert), Small Press Traffic, Tucson Museum of Art, Center for Book Arts (w/ Joey De Jesus), GUEST (w/ Brenda Iijima), the *Colorado Review,* and Split This Rock's Poem of the Week series.

To the following individuals and institutions for offering me space and dollars: Headlands Center for the Arts; Dawn Lundy Martin, Angie Cruz, Lauren Russell, and the Center for African American Poetry and Poetics at the University of Pittsburgh; Oak Spring Garden Foundation; Hanif Abdurraqib and the Virginia Piper Center for Creative Writing at Arizona State University; Sarah Riggs and Tamaass Cross Cultural Organization, Arizona Commission on the Arts; Mahogany Brown and Just Media; t'ai freedom ford and PowerHouse Residency.

For years of thinking, feeling, reading, snacking, walking, weeding, car-assing, crying, and questioning alongside me: Keeonna Harris, Tonya Foster, Nicole Sealey, Christine Allen-Blanchette, Kaneza Schaal, t'ai freedom ford, Latasha N. Nevada Diggs, Abou Farman, Muriel Leung, Christina Olivares, Amanda Tachine, Douglas Kearney, Ariel Goldberg, Catie Moore, Youna Kwak, Benjamin Krusling, Jo Wu, and Ellen Pierce, thank you.

For Tuesdays. And listening together. For the ways that you show me myself. Thank you, Ica.

To my first teachers: Ellis Avery and Marcellus Blount, thank you.

Deep gratitude to the writers and artists whose works move me toward the language I need, especially: Etel Adnan, Dionne Brand, Beverly Buchanan, Suzanne Césaire, Dolores Dorantes, Cristina Rivera Garza, Renee Gladman, Fred Moten, Alejandra Pizarnik, Hortense Spillers, and Sylvia Wynter.

To these organizations and communities for making some deep listening and healing possible: No More Deaths PHX; About Face: Veterans Against the War; Freedom Fighter Gun and Safety Club; Red Lake Treaty Camp; Mariposas sin Fronteras; and Earthseed and the Native Health Phoenix Community Garden, thank you.

To my parents, Wendy Jo and Henry John, for getting me this far; my sisters, Syrita and Amanda, for insisting on joy in the process, thank you.

For moving with me through many ways of love, and for opening corners of your desert, thank you, Natalie—you made this book possible.

Coffee House Press began as a small letterpress operation in 1972 and has grown into an internationally renowned nonprofit publisher of literary fiction, essay, poetry, and other work that doesn't fit neatly into genre categories.

Coffee House is both a publisher and an arts organization. Through our *Books in Action* program and publications, we've become interdisciplinary collaborators and incubators for new work and audience experiences. Our vision for the future is one where a publisher is a catalyst and connector.

LITERATURE
is not the same thing as
PUBLISHING

Funder Acknowledgments

Coffee House Press is an internationally renowned independent book publisher and arts nonprofit based in Minneapolis, MN; through its literary publications and *Books in Action* program, Coffee House acts as a catalyst and connector—between authors and readers, ideas and resources, creativity and community, inspiration and action.

Coffee House Press books are made possible through the generous support of grants and donations from corporations, state and federal grant programs, family foundations, and the many individuals who believe in the transformational power of literature. This activity is made possible by the voters of Minnesota through a Minnesota State Arts Board Operating Support grant, thanks to the legislative appropriation from the Arts and Cultural Heritage Fund. Coffee House also receives major operating support from the Amazon Literary Partnership, Jerome Foundation, Literary Arts Emergency Fund, McKnight Foundation, and the National Endowment for the Arts (NEA). To find out more about how NEA grants impact individuals and communities, visit www.arts.gov.

Coffee House Press receives additional support from Bookmobile; the Buckley Charitable Fund; Dorsey & Whitney LLP; the Gaea Foundation; the Schwab Charitable Fund; and the U.S. Bank Foundation.

The Publisher's Circle of Coffee House Press

Publisher's Circle members make significant contributions to Coffee House Press's annual giving campaign. Understanding that a strong financial base is necessary for the press to meet the challenges and opportunities that arise each year, this group plays a crucial part in the success of Coffee House's mission.

Recent Publisher's Circle members include many anonymous donors, Kathy Arnold, Patricia A. Beithon, Andrew Brantingham & Rita Farmer, Kelli & Dave Cloutier, Theodore Cornwell, Mary Ebert & Paul Stembler, Kamilah Foreman, Eva Galiber, Jocelyn Hale & Glenn Miller Charitable Fund of the Minneapolis Foundation, Roger Hale & Nor Hall, William Hardacker, Randy Hartten & Ron Lotz, Carl & Heidi Horsch, Amy L. Hubbard & Geoffrey J. Kehoe Fund of the St. Paul & Minnesota Foundation, Kenneth & Susan Kahn, the Kenneth Koch Literary Estate, Cinda Kornblum, the Lenfestey Family Foundation, Sarah Lutman & Rob Rudolph, Carol & Aaron Mack, Gillian McCain, Mary & Malcolm McDermid, Daniel N. Smith III & Maureen Millea Smith, Vance Opperman, Mr. Pancks' Fund in memory of Graham Kimpton, Alan Polsky, Robin Preble, Steve Smith, Paul Thissen, Grant Wood, and Margaret Wurtele.

For more information about the Publisher's Circle and other ways to support Coffee House Press books, authors, and activities, please visit www.coffeehousepress.org/pages/donate or contact us at info@coffeehousepress.org.

COFFEE HOUSE PRESS began as a small letterpress operation in 1972. In the years since, it has grown into an internationally renowned nonprofit publisher of literary fiction, nonfiction, poetry, and other writing that doesn't fit neatly into genre categories. Our mission is to expand definitions of what literature can be, what it can do, and to whom it belongs.

FURTHER POETRY TITLES FROM COFFEE HOUSE PRESS

For more information about Coffee House Press and how you can support our mission, please visit coffeehousepress.org/pages/donate

Professors may request desk copies by visiting coffeehousepress.org/pages/educators

SARETTA MORGAN was born in Appalachia and raised on military instal-
lations. She's interested in the ecologies and intimacies that materialize in
the shadows of US militarization. She is a member of the Belladonna*
Collaborative and organizes with the grassroots humanitarian aid organi-
zation No More Deaths, and with About Face: Veterans Against the War.

Alt-Nature was designed by
Bookmobile Design & Digital Publisher Services.
Text is set in Adobe Garamond Pro.